T0024552

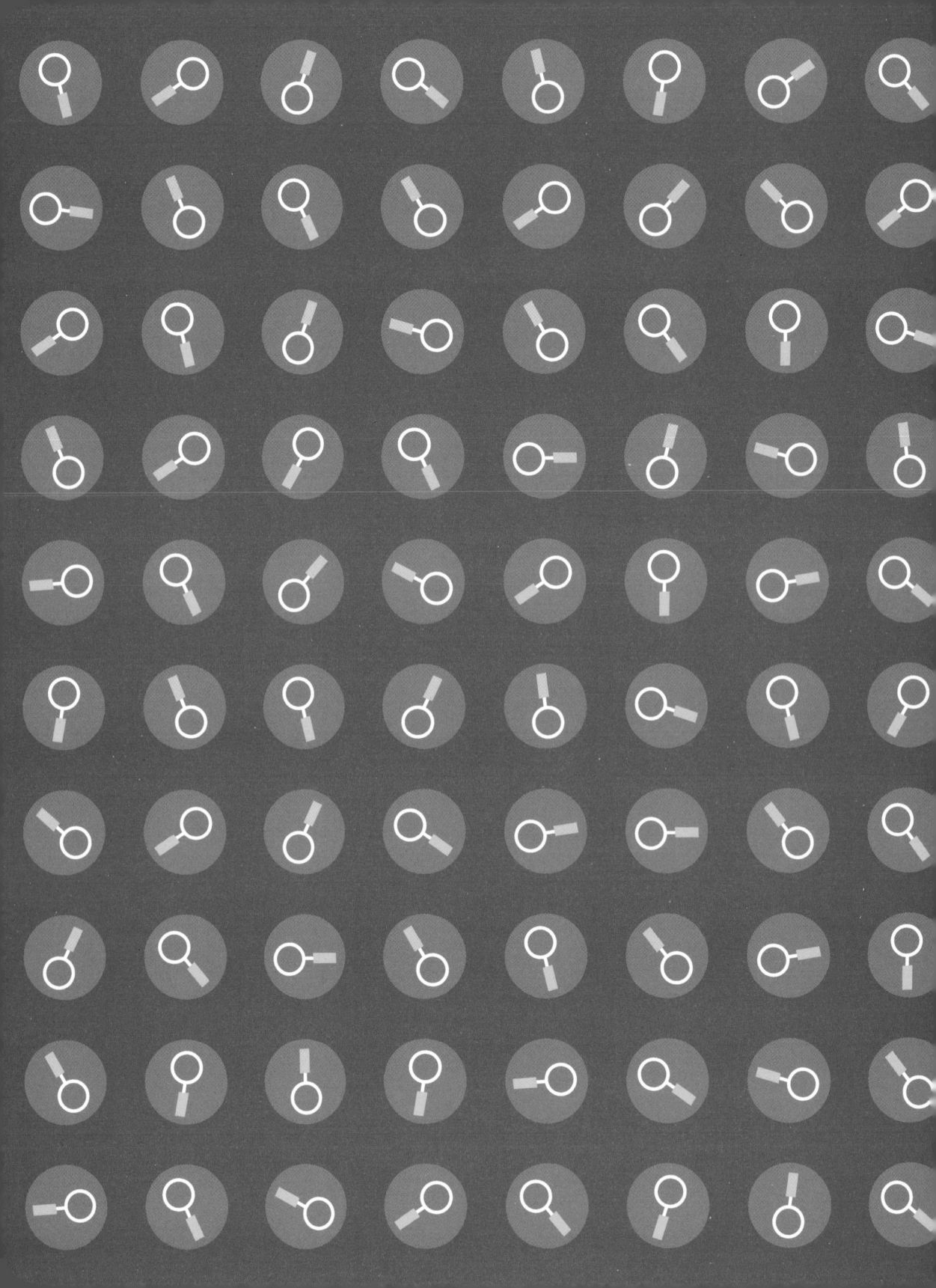

Spot the Differences

ADORABLE ANIMALS

By Sarah Parvis and Georgia Rucker

PBS KIDS and the PBS KIDS logo are registered marks of the Public Broadcasting Service. Used with permission. © 2019 PBS. All rights reserved.

100% of the net proceeds PBS KIDS receives from your purchase of this book supports the mission of PBS.

www.pbskids.org

downtown bookworks

Downtown Bookworks Inc.
265 Canal Street, New York, NY 10013

Copyright © 2019 by Downtown Bookworks Inc.

By Sarah Parvis
Designed by Georgia Rucker
Printed in China, June 2019

10 9 8 7 6 5 4 3 2 1

All rights reserved. No part of this book may be reproduced in any form or by any means without prior written permission from the publisher.

PHOTO CREDITS Front cover: Katho Menden/Shutterstock.com (dogs), ©iStock.com/proxyminder (butterfly), ©iStock.com/colevineyard (tennis ball), Oksana Kuzmina/Shutterstock.com (cat). Interior: 1: tristan tan/Shutterstock.com (orangutans), Richard Peterson/Shutterstock.com (recorder), David Carillet/Shutterstock.com (eye patch), Levchenko Ilia/Shutterstock.com (ice cream). 3: Duplass/Shutterstock.com (boy), cellistka/Shutterstock.com (new snake), fivespots/Shutterstock.com (tail). 4–5: SaNa/Shutterstock.com. 5: Rudmer Zwerver/Shutterstock.com (mouse). 6–7: Vaclav Sebek/Shutterstock.com. 7: Mike Truchon/Shutterstock.com (bird), Katrina Leigh/Shutterstock.com (yo-yo), Sergey Mironov/Shutterstock.com (backpack). 8: Mogens Trolle/Shutterstock.com (elephants), Thitisan/Shutterstock.com (hot-air balloon), Eric Aust/Shutterstock.com (trunk), Susan Schmitz/Shutterstock.com (hat), Marques/Shutterstock.com (rubber duck). 9: yevgeniy11/Shutterstock.com (pigs on fence, piglet), Nadia Cruzova/Shutterstock.com (bracelet), nikolansfoto/Shutterstock (dartboard), Alis Photo/Shutterstock.com (horseshoe). 10: vladsilver/Shutterstock.com (penguins), Timof/Shutterstock.com (snowman), Vilvarin/Shutterstock.com (bow tie), mikeledray/Shutterstock.com (top hat), OLGA ALEXANDROVA/Shutterstock.com (rabbit). 11: Olga Kot Photo/Shutterstock.com (llama), FocusStocker/Shutterstock.com (soccer ball), snowturtle/Shutterstock.com (cable cars). 12: Oksana Kuzmina/Shutterstock.com (cat, new cat), Dado Photos/Shutterstock.com (flamingo and flowers). 13: CamPix Prints/Shutterstock.com (farm), photomaster/Shutterstock.com (duck), Maria Maheras/Shutterstock.com (sunglasses), Diane Garcia/Shutterstock.com (smiley face). 14: Julee75/Shutterstock.com (meerkats, new meerkat), Madlen/Shutterstock.com (bow tie), Elena Kharichkina/Shutterstock.com (wig). 15: Mike Truchon/Shutterstock.com (oriole), Beautiful landscape/Shutterstock.com (whole orange), Evgeny Karandaev/Shutterstock.com (berries). 16: ©Klaus Tiedge/Blend Images/SuperStock (seal), triptheanchor/Shutterstock.com (buoy), Mangostar/Shutterstock.com (camera), Sean Locke Photography/Shutterstock.com (foam finger). 17: ©iStock.com/Liliboas (dog), Ulrich Willmunder/Shutterstock.com (bone), Michael Kraus/Shutterstock.com (pin). 18: Ondrej Prosicky/Shutterstock.com (panda), Elnur/Shutterstock.com (crown), asharkyu/Shutterstock.com (party horn, birdhouse). 19: LightField Studios/Shutterstock.com (dog, picture in frame), Anton27/Shutterstock.com (cat), Iakov Filimonov/Shutterstock.com (frame), Chani Friedman/Shutterstock.com (doll). 20: dimmitrius/Shutterstock.com (swans), Artem Avetisyan/Shutterstock.com (bow tie), Yakov Oskanov/Shutterstock.com (hippo), Alberto Masnovo/Shutterstock.com (buoy line). 21: tristan tan/Shutterstock.com (orangutans), Richard Peterson/Shutterstock.com (recorder), David Carillet/Shutterstock.com (eye patch), Levchenko Ilia/Shutterstock.com (ice cream). 22: Marvin Minder/Shutterstock.com (sloth), Kanea/Shutterstock.com (leaf), Tim UR/Shutterstock.com (apple), Joe Belanger/Shutterstock.com (bread). 23: Elizaveta Galitckaia/Shutterstock.com (boy), cigdem/Shutterstock.com (propeller), Megan Betteridge/Shutterstock.com (bandanna), oksana2010/Shutterstock.com (new goats). 24: seasoning_17/Shutterstock.com (turtles, hatching turtle), RATCHANAT BUA-NGERN/Shutterstock.com (marble). 25: ©iStock.com/ngung (parrots), vvoe/Shutterstock.com (paintbrush), Roman Samborskyi/Shutterstock.com (medal). 26: ©iStock.com/sbossert (chipmunk), Abel Tumik/Shutterstock.com (seeds), Mountain Light Studios/Shutterstock.com (chair), weerawath.p/Shutterstock.com (lights). 27: Bachkova Natalia/Shutterstock.com (birds), LAURA_VN/Shutterstock.com (berries), photomaster/Shutterstock.com (flying bird). 28: evakad17/Shutterstock.com (hamster cage, hamster house), prapann/Shutterstock.com (sign). 29: Jez Bennett/Shutterstock.com (lemur), Goran Bogicevic/Shutterstock.com (tambourine), davidek1/Shutterstock.com (moon). 30: Edmund O'Connor/Shutterstock.com (iguana), Susan Schmitz/Shutterstock.com (cape), Francisco Amaral Leitao/Shutterstock.com (totem), soportography/Shutterstock.com (parasailers). 31: Volodymyr Burdiak/Shutterstock.com (giraffes, new giraffe), Grushin/Shutterstock.com (binoculars), BlueOrange Studio/Shutterstock.com (tire swing). 32: hedgehog111/Shutterstock.com (all). 33: Dirima/Shutterstock.com (puppy), Africa Studio (pineapple), Kletr/Shutterstock.com (snorkel), Butterfly Hunter/Shutterstock.com (butterfly). 34: frantisekhojdysz/Shutterstock.com (yellow fish), Alena Ohneva/Shutterstock.com (bubbles), Gerald Robert Fischer/Shutterstock.com (new coral). 35: ©iStock.com/ivanmateev (leopard), Praisaeng/Shutterstock.com (turtle), Jules_Kitano/Shutterstock.com (sailboat). 36: Maria Dryfhout/Shutterstock.com (deer), Normana Karia/Shutterstock.com (wreath), Vastram/Shutterstock.com (pine cones), Kitch Bain/Shutterstock.com (jelly beans), Constantin Iosif/Shutterstock.com (feather). 37: ichywong/Shutterstock.com (zebra), Dirk M. de Boer/Shutterstock.com (yellow bird). 38–39: Gerald A. DeBoer/Shutterstock.com. 39: NuttoKung/Shutterstock.com (leaves), AnnaDona/Shutterstock.com (yellow eyes), Peyker/Shutterstock.com (clown nose), Levent Konuk/Shutterstock.com (caterpillar). 40: Natalia Barsukova/Shutterstock.com (flamingos), Michael Kraus/Shutterstock.com (plastic flamingo), Elena Yakusheva/Shutterstock.com (mermaid). 41: Kandarp/Shutterstock.com (peacock), sportoakimirka/Shutterstock.com (birdie), Dario Lo Presti/Shutterstock.com (billiard ball), wedninth/Shutterstock.com (spoon), Dan Thornberg/Shutterstock.com (baseball). 42: Ondrej Prosicky/Shutterstock.com (toucan), Dirk Ercken/Shutterstock.com (frog), Sangaroon/Shutterstock.com (flower). 43: skvalval/Shutterstock.com (trainer), Africa Studio/Shutterstock.com (gum), A_Lesik/Shutterstock.com (audience), New Africa/Shutterstock.com (float). 44: yana_vinnikova/Shutterstock.com (rabbits), Brittany Lillegard/Shutterstock.com (flowers), Anna Aibetova/Shutterstock.com (clover), BERNATSKAYA OXANA/Shutterstock.com (ants). 45: A3pfamily/Shutterstock.com (deer), Cherednichenko Aleksandr/Shutterstock.com (bow), WilleeCole Photography/Shutterstock.com (wand), Punchalit Chotiksatian/Shutterstock.com (lei), Paul Tessier/Shutterstock.com (tail). 46–47: lunamarina/Shutterstock.com. 47: Dima Moroz/Shutterstock.com (curtains), Olhastock/Shutterstock.com (new chicken), Luis Molinero/Shutterstock.com (door handle), Africa Studio/Shutterstock.com (chick). 48: Kletr/Shutterstock.com (all). 49: alexei_tm/Shutterstock.com (dog, closed window), ©iStock.com/seewhatmitchsee (chimney). 50–51: Sinisa Botas/Shutterstock.com. 51: Marsan/Shutterstock.com (knight), Ad Oculos/Shutterstock.com (crab), Africa Studio/Shutterstock.com (headphones). 52: Susan Kehoe/Shutterstock.com (bears), Alrandir/Shutterstock.com (birdbath), tuasiwatn/Shutterstock.com (earmuffs), Christopher MacDonald/Shutterstock.com (bear cub), sumroeng chinnapan/Shutterstock.com (pool). 53: galitsin/Shutterstock.com (kids), modus_vivendi/Shutterstock.com (pig statue), Phichai/Shutterstock.com (headband), pullia/Shutterstock.com (flower), Oleinik Iuliia/Shutterstock.com (face paint). 54: reisegraf.ch/Shutterstock.com (iguana), Super Prin/Shutterstock.com (fish), reisegraf.ch/Shutterstock.com (new bird), BlueOrange Studio/Shutterstock.com (crab). 55: Stephen Clarke/Shutterstock.com (frogs), Humannet/Shutterstock.com (pink petal), irin-k/Shutterstock.com (ladybug), kazoka/Shutterstock.com (frog leg). 56: Anton27/Shutterstock.com (cat), Voronin76/Shutterstock.com (tie). 57: horsemen/Shutterstock.com (horse jump), Sittirak Jadlit/Shutterstock.com (helmet), Gcapture/Shutterstock.com (blue pole), Mega Pixel/Shutterstock.com (peppermint), Eric Isselee/Shutterstock.com (gray horse). Back cover: Julee75/Shutterstock.com (meerkats, new meerkat), Madlen/Shutterstock.com (bow tie), Elena Kharichkina/Shutterstock.com (wig).

Spot the Differences

Look at each pair of pictures. Point at everything that is different. And count the differences you find.

Hi, parents! As your kids do these puzzles, tell them to look out for:

- **items that have appeared or disappeared**
- **things that have gotten larger or smaller or shorter or longer**
- **colors that have changed**
- **objects that have been replaced with something new**

If your child is stumped, remind them to look closely at each picture and see how they are different.

You can even ask questions to help.
Do the boy's shoes look the same in each picture?
How many snakes are in each picture?
Is there something different about his shirt?

This number tells you how many differences are in the puzzle.

The puzzles get more challenging as you go!

Spot the differences puzzles are a great workout for visual observation and spatial relations skills. Encourage your child to celebrate each find by saying what they spotted aloud. Naming objects, colors, and size differences will also boost your child's vocabulary and confidence—plus, it's fun!

Kitty Catch

Point to **4** differences

Fox in the Field

Point to **4** differences

Elephant Fun!

Point to **4** differences

Pig Pals

Point to **4** differences

Penguins on Parade

Point to **4** differences

Sightseeing Llama

Point to **4** differences

Kitty's Playhouse

Point to **4** differences

Donkey in the Barnyard

Point to **4** differences

Meerkat Meeting

Point to **4** differences

Oriole at the Bird Feeder

Point to **4** differences

Seal by the Sea

Point to **4** differences

Puppy Spa Day

Point to **4** differences

Happy Panda

Point to **4** differences

Super Buddies!

Point to **4** differences

Swan Lake

Point to **4** differences

Orangutans Hanging Out

Point to **4** differences

Sloth Picnic

Point to **4** differences

Hello, Little Goat!

Point to **4** differences

Welcome, Baby Turtles!

Point to **4** differences

Five Colorful Parrots

Point to **4** differences

Chipmunks Love Seeds

Point to **4** differences

Birds on the Lookout

Point to **4** differences

squeaky

Leaping Lemur!

Point to **4** differences

Iguana Vacation

Point to **4** differences

Giraffes on Safari

Point to **4** differences

Hedgehog on a Ledge

Point to **4** differences

Puppy at the Pool

Point to **4** differences

Something's Fishy

Point to **4** differences

Thirsty Leopard

Point to **4** differences

Deer Meets Snowman

Point to **5** differences

Zebra Stripes

Point to **5** differences

Raccoon Den

Point to **5** differences

SD
+
VK

Flamingo Beach Party

Point to **5** differences

Fabulous Peacock Feathers

Point to **5** differences

Toucan in a Tree

Point to **5** differences

Dolphin Training Day

Point to **5** differences

Cuddle-Bunnies

Point to **5** differences

Forest Friends

Point to **5** differences

Chicken Coop

Point to **5** differences

Colorful Clownfish

Point to **5** differences

Come Over to Rover's

Point to **5** differences

Welcome to Fish Castle

Point to **5** differences

Bear With Us

Point to **5** differences

Piggy Takes a Nap

Point to **5** differences

Iguana in the Sun

Point to **5** differences

Sunflower Frogs

Point to **5** differences

That's Not a Bunny!

Point to **6** differences

Horse Jump

Point to **6** differences

Answer Key

front cover

p. 3

p. 4–5

p. 6–7

p. 8

p. 9

p. 10

p. 11

p. 12

p. 13

p. 14

p. 15

p. 16

p. 17

p. 18

Answer Key

p. 19

p. 20

p. 21

p. 22

p. 23

p. 24

p. 25

p. 26

p. 27

p. 28

p. 29

p. 30

p. 31

p. 32

p. 33

p. 34

Answer Key

p. 35

p. 36

p. 37

p. 38–39

p. 40

p. 41

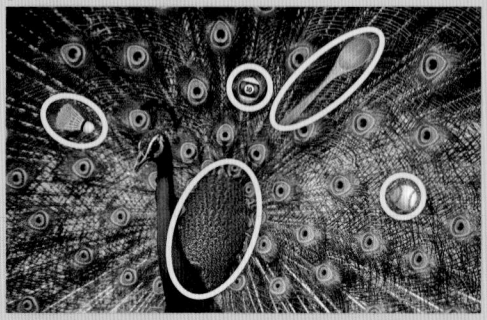

p. 42

p. 43

p. 44

p. 45

p. 46–47

p. 48

p. 49

p. 50–51

p. 52

Answer Key

p. 53

p. 54

p. 55

p. 56

p. 57

Special thanks to all our puzzle testers and their helpers: Joanna Schlesser-Perry, Kai Schlesser, and Aiden Williams; Christina and Vincent Vermillion; Selina Greene and Oliver Cooper; Bryan Giansanti and Hollis and Harper Giansanti Stokes; Lana, Carter, and Mona O'Brien; Josiah and Davis Trager; Sarah, Jameson, and Annabelle Tormey; Nana and Archer Skye Lamouse-Welch; Eliana Doft and Judith and Nate Ottensoser; and Ari Barbanell Kassirer and Ellington Kassirer.

Don't miss the other book in the series!

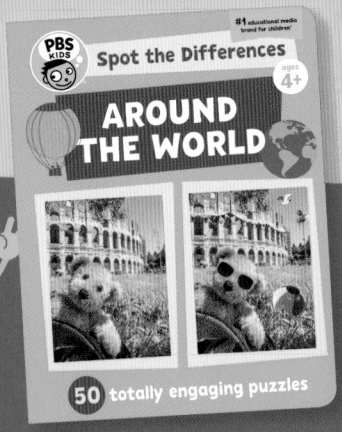

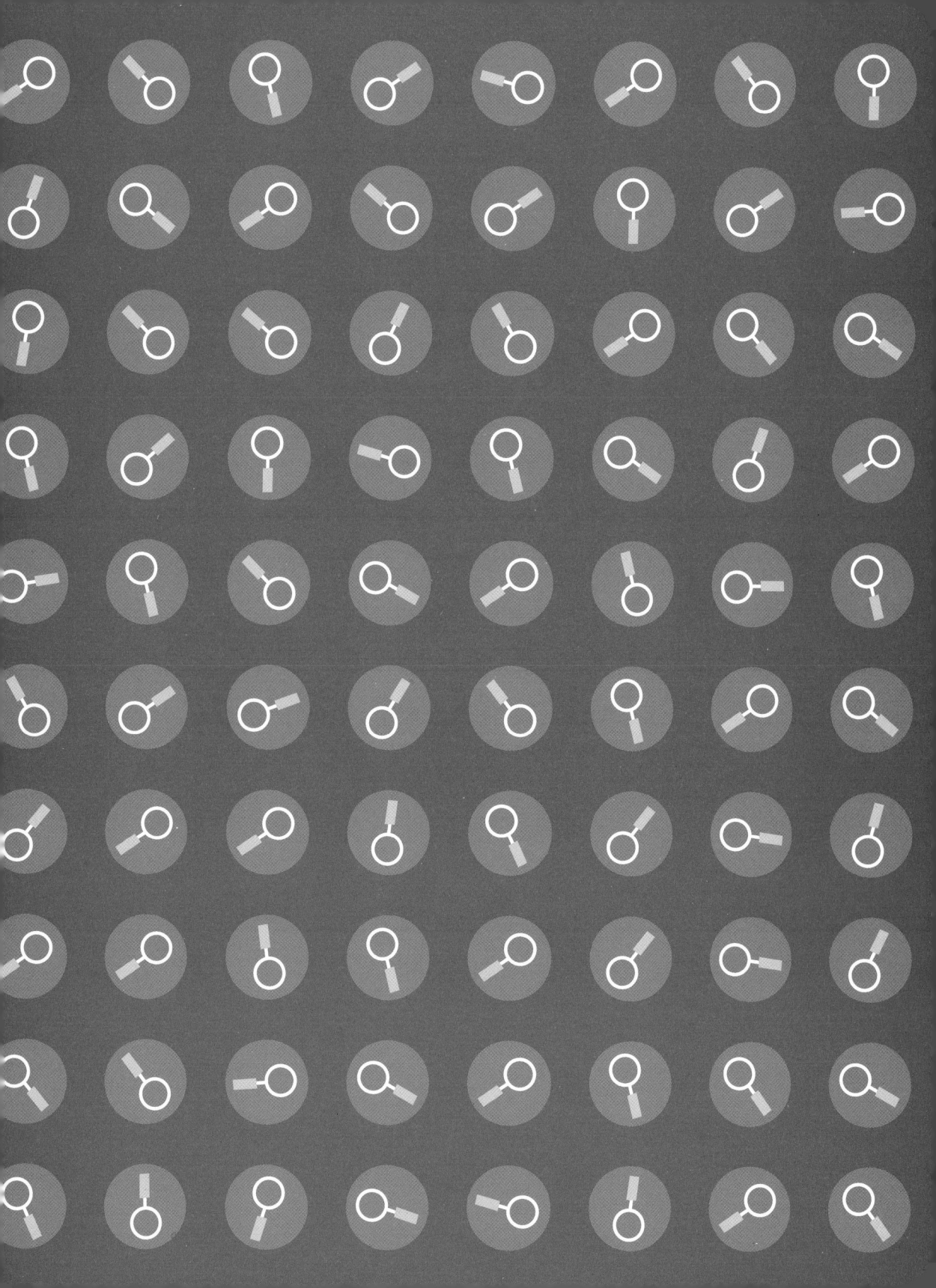